HOW TO CREATE YOUR OWN SELF DIRECTED CHECKBOOK IRA FOR REAL ESTATE INVESTING IN 8 EASY STEPS

HAVE YOUR LLC UP AND RUNNING IN JUST A FEW WEEKS

ROBIN WISEMAN

INTRODUCTION

Disclaimer: These instructions are for company creation in the State of Georgia. You'll need to do a little bit more research to learn and/or confirm the set up when creating in a different state.

Are you in the real estate business and tired of letting someone else choose how your investment account is handled? In less than two years, I have more than doubled my initial investment portfolio and am now sharing how I did it.

After contributing to a corporate world 401k for about 15 years, watching it's value rise and fall with each stock market scare, I had the opportunity to leave that type of work life behind, get my real estate license and work for myself as an independent contractor. Now came my dilemma of what to do with that money in the hands of the investment firm hired by my former employer that just seemed to be sitting there not making anywhere the amount of money I'd need for my golden retirement age. Like many, life got in the way and I really didn't start thinking about investing in my old age until I was my 30's and here I was in my early 50's with not nearly the amount I knew would be necessary to comfortably survive while looking at still making a mortgage payment until I was 65. Who wants that? Not me. So my research began into just how I could manage that money myself. Research...research...research! This booklet contains, step by step, my path to success in creating a Single Member Managed LLC / Domestic Limited Liability Company in the State of Georgia. I've no doubt this process can be applied to other states and will be of great assistance to do your own research and tweak it as necessary.

First...you're going to need capital if you want to invest in something. If you have a nice fat bank account or wealthy relatives to assist and just want to know how to start the ball rolling, let's roll! For me, upon leaving my former employer, I had the opportunity to roll an existing 401k with them over to a new employer, a private managed investment company or just take the tax hit, withdraw it and blow it on whatever my heart desired. I was also welcome to just let it sit where it was at and continue the measly annual gains I'd witnessed over the years. The value of it at that time was about $48K. None of those available options were desireable to me. Why should I let an investment company continue to make money off of my money? I decided it was time to set up my own company. Overcome fears. Do it. Take that existing 401K and roll it over to a Traditional IRA that was self directed. My overly cautious, play it safe, personality had to be overcome. Take a deep breath. Ready, Set, GO!

Are YOU ready? If so, grab a three ring binder and some plastic page sleeves to place all your info in as you follow these steps. Stay organized and focused and you can have this all taken care of in your spare time over a couple of weeks.

STEP 1

CREATE YOUR COMPANY NAME

Figure out what you want to name your company. Hop online at: https://ecorp.sos.ga.gov/ Click that Online Services button and create a user account. Once that's set up, follow their online instructions to create & register your company. I created a Domestic Limited Liability Company. Grab your credit card and pay the $100 fee and click enter. You'll get an email back from the state shortly. Start an electronic folder on your PC desktop or in the Cloud, save an electronic copy of the letter and print out a copy to make it the first page in your new 3 ring binder. You will need to pay an annual registration fee of $50 to renew the business each year thereafter.

STATE OF GEORGIA
Secretary of State
Corporations Division
313 West Tower
2 Martin Luther King, Jr. Dr.
Atlanta, Georgia 30334-1530

Secretary of State, Brian P. Kemp

Billing Information

GA30281, USA

Product Description	Receipt Number	Order Date	Item Cost	Expedited	Total
Business Formation LLC Control #: Shipped via: Online		/2015	$100.00	$0.00	$100.00

Invoice Total: $100.00

Payment Information
Payment for $100.00 from Web with Credit Card - VISA

Payment Address

Control Number: 15

STATE OF GEORGIA
Secretary of State
Corporation: Division
313 West Tower
2 Martin Luther King, Jr. Dr.
Atlanta, Georgia 30334-1530

CERTIFICATE OF ORGANIZATION

I, Brian P. Kemp, the Secretary of State and the Corporation Commissioner of the State of Georgia, hereby certify under the seal of my office that

LLC

a Domestic Limited Liability Company

has been duly organized under the laws of the State of Georgia on /2015 by the filing of articles of organization in the Office of the Secretary of State and by the paying of fees as provided by Title 14 of the Official Code of Georgia Annotated.

WITNESS my hand and official seal in the City of Atlanta
and the State of Georgia on 09/31/2015

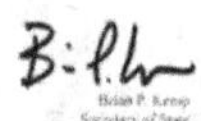

Brian P. Kemp
Secretary of State

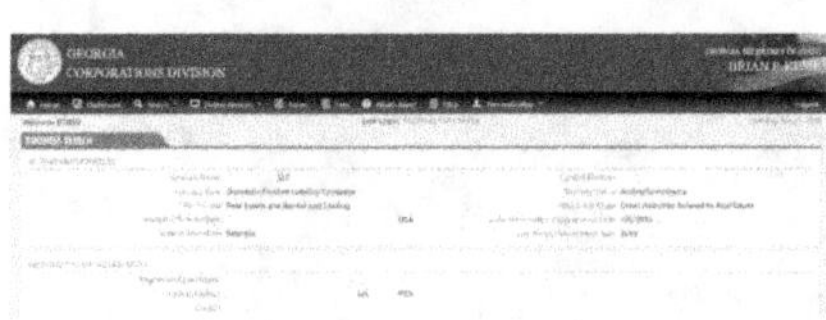

2

———

STEP 2

GET YOUR EIN FROM THE IRS

Next, you'll need to request an EIN number from the IRS for your business. hop online at: https://www.irs.gov/businesses/small-businesses-self-employed/apply-for-an-employer-identification-number-ein-online Just follow the online instructions and once completed, you'll receive an email from the the IRS issuing your new EIN number. Save an electronic copy of the letter and print that bad boy out and put it in your binder.

Congratulations!

You now own a company. Those two steps shouldn't have taken more than an hour, at most, of your time to take care of and I just saved you a couple hundred bucks from those online companies like legal zoom that want to charge various fees + get all your personal information to do something that, seriously now, just took you minutes to do yourself. Your welcome. Now comes the tasks that will take a bit more of your time.

3

———

STEP 3

CHOOSE A COMPANY TO REPRESENT YOUR EQUITY

Choose an authorized company to represent your private equity. That company will track your portfolio, require fair market value reports of your assets annually, and report those findings to the IRS. Choosing such a company entailed a lot of research and I settled with a company out of Kentucky called Kingdom Trust. My IRA set up entailed the rollover of funds from a corporate 401k or I would face tax ramifications by receiving said funds, so they needed to be transferred directly into such a company as this. There was an initial $125 account set up fee and then there's an annual administrative fee of about the same amount each year.

4

———

STEP 4

COMPANY OPERATING AGREEMENT

Now the hardest thing...creating and writing your own company operating agreement. You can pay an attorney thousands of dollars to write up a customized operating agreement or you can simply plagairize my single member managed one and tweak it to be your own. I'm about to save you weeks worth of pondering, stress, headaches and keyboard work. Your operating agreement must be consistent with the type of business you have created. Keep in mind, you can't properly create this until you have completed the prior work in the proceeding Steps.

AUTHOR DISCLOSURE: QUOTED TAX LAWS AND / OR CODE NUMBERS COULD CHANGE. WHAT IS NOTED IN THIS EXAMPLE WERE IN AFFECT IN 2015. YOU MUST DO YOUR OWN DUE DILIGENCE AND VERIFY ACCURACY OF CURRENT CODES, IF NECESSARY.

Now...if you've read this far, wouldn't it be nice to have the following document in a nice, editable Word format? Just copy and paste!

Here goes!

Operating Agreement of
XYZ LLC
A Georgia Single Member Managed
Limited Liability Company

THE MEMBERSHIP INTERESTS EVIDENCED BY THIS AGREEMENT HAVE NOT BEEN REGISTERED UNDER THE SECURITIES ACT OF 1933, AS AMENDED, OR UNDER THE SECURITIES LAWS OF ANY STATE OR FOREIGN JURISDICTION AND MAY NOT BE SOLD OR TRANSFERRED WITHOUT COMPLIANCE WITH ANY AND ALL APPLICABLE FEDERAL, STATE OR FOREIGN SECURITIES LAWS.

Table of Contents

CONTENTS SAMPLE

Operating Agreement of
XYZ LLC
(A Single Member Managed Limited Liability Company)

This Operating Agreement of XYZ LLC (A Limited Liability Company), is entered into as of the date set forth in Article XVII Signatures of Members and Managers, by and among, the undersigned as "Members" or "Managers"

WHEREAS, the LLC has been formed by filing Articles of Organization with the Georgia Secretary of State. A copy of this Organizational Document is placed in the LLC's records and available online at: https://ecorp.sos.ga.gov

NOW, THEREFORE, in consideration of the mutual covenants herein contained, the parties hereto, intending to be legally bound, agree and certify as follows:

Article I
Name

The name of the Limited Liability Company shall be XYZ LLC.

Article II
Principal Place of Business

2.1 The location of the principal place of business shall be:

123 Main Street Anytown GA 12345

Article III
Registered Agent

3.1 The registered agent for this LLC is:

(Your name here)

Article IV
Purpose of LLC

4.1 The specific purpose of the LLC shall include the following, as amended, adopted, and exempted by the Internal Revenue Code Section 4975(a) and Department of Labor PTE 96-62:

4.1.1 <u>Real Estate</u>: Buy, sell, mortgage, encumber, develop, lease, invest in, deal in, and otherwise hold undeveloped, community, residential, and agricultural, real and personal property of all kinds.

4.1.2 <u>Deeds of Trusts and Mortgages</u>: To invest in deeds of trusts, mortgage notes and other interest-bearing notes, whether in first or subordinate positions, and whether purchased from brokers or private parties. To purchase discounted notes and real estate purchase options.

4.1.3 <u>Additionally</u>, the LLC may acquire such assets and engage in investments of all types and any and all other lawful purposes that may be conducted by a LLC as deemed appropriate by the Manager. However, the business and purpose of the LLC shall not be limited to its initial principal business activity and it shall have authority to engage in any other lawful business, trade, purpose or activity permitted by the Act, and it shall possess and may exercise all of the powers and privileges granted by the Act or which the manager deems appropriate.

Article V
General Authority of the LLC

The General Authority of the LLC shall be as follows:

5.1.1 To operate for the exclusive benefit of the member and/or its beneficiaries, pursuant to Internal Revenue Code Section 408(a) and as further defined in Internal Revenue Publication 590, section 2.

5.1.2 To derive income from regularly carried on trades or business that substantially relate to the performance by the LLC in fulfillment of its exempt purpose, to operate for the exclusive benefit of the member and/or its beneficiaries.

5.1.3 To expend LLC capital and income in the exercise of any of their rights or powers hereunder;

5.1.4 To purchase, sell, assign, convey or otherwise transfer title to any portion of the LLC's real and personal property, including any interest in any mortgage, lease, or other interest in real or personal property;

5.1.5 To lease, upon such terms as may be deemed proper, all or any portion of the LLC's real or personal property, regardless of whether the leased space or facility is to be occupied by the lessee or subleased in whole or in part to others;

5.1.6 To borrow money for the LLC on the security of all or any part of its real and personal property, and in conjunction therewith, execute all the necessary papers and documents, including, but not limited to, bonds, notes, mortgages, security agreements, and confessions of judgment for and on behalf of the LLC;

5.1.7 To obtain replacements of mortgages of the LLC's property;

5.1.8 To prepay in whole or in part, refinance, increase, modify, consolidate, or extend, on such terms as the Manager may deem proper, any debts affecting the LLC's real or personal property;

5.1.9 To place record title to the LLC's real or personal property in the name or names of a nominee or nominees for the purpose of mortgage financing or any other convenience or benefit to the LLC, so long as such action does not create a non-exempted prohibited transaction as defined in section 4975 of the Internal Revenue Code;

5.1.10 To set aside LLC capital or other funds for payment of past, current, and future liabilities of the LLC;

5.1.11 To select and open LLC bank accounts, and withdrawals there from to be make upon a signature by the Manager;

5.1.12 To invest as a Member in any property and make supplemental investments in and/or loans to other entities and to take any action to protect the LLC's investments, in their sold discretion, including, without limitation, the right to vote on all matters requiring the votes of the LLC under any investment;

5.1.13 To lend money or extend credit on behalf of the LLC;

5.1.14 To invest and reinvest LLC funds;

5.1.15 To hypothecate securities owned by the LLC;

5.1.16 To incur obligations (contractual or otherwise), and to perform, compromise, or discharge such obligations;

5.1.17 To retain other persons, firms or corporations to render services to them or to the LLC and to compensate such persons, firms or corporation therefore;

5.1.18 To subject to their continuing general supervision, to delegate to other Persons the performance of any duties they are required to perform or the exercise of any rights they possess;

5.1.19 To prosecute, defend, or compromise actions on behalf of the LLC;

5.1.20 To become a Manager or Member in another LLC;

5.1.21 To exercise all voting and other rights incident to the LLC's ownership of an interest in another Person;

5.1.22 To pay or reimburse any Person for costs, expenses, or losses incurred in connection with any aspect of the LLC or its business;

5.1.23 To do and perform all such other acts as may be necessary or appropriate to the conduct of the LLC's business;

5.1.24 To negotiate for, execute and conclude agreements for the sale, exchange, or other disposition of all or substantially all of the property of the LLC as provided for herein;

5.1.25 To establish and maintain appropriate reserves for expenses, losses, and liabilities, contingent or otherwise; and

5.1.26 To not engage in any of the aforementioned activities, if by taking such action there would be a violation of sections 408 or 4975 of the Internal Revenue Code, not exempted by Department of Labor PTE 96-62.

Article VI
Capital Contributions of Members

6.1 Member: The member of the LLC shall be The Kingdom Trust Company, Custodian FBO, (your name here) IRA (number here).

6.2. Initial Capital Contributions: The initial capital contributions contributed by the Member and the fair market values thereof as represented by Interests in the LLC are listed on Schedule B attached hereto.

6.2.3 Additional Capital Contributions: Except as may be required by Internal Revenue Code 704, and except as otherwise determined by the Manager, no additional share of Profits or Losses shall inure to any Member because of changes or fluctuations in his or her capital account.

6.2.4 Revaluations under Certain Circumstances: The value of property contributed by the Members has been agreed to by each Member. The Interests of this LLC have been allocated based on such valuation and are deemed equal to the capital contributed. If a valuation different from that agreed is finally determined by the

Internal Revenue Service, then the percentage ownership of the LLC Interests ma in the sole discretion of the Manager, be increased or decreased, as may be appropriate, so the at the fair market value of the Member's contributed capital as of the date of contribution. If such reallocation of LLC Interests requires a redetermination and reallocation of profits, losses, and cash distributed, then each Member shall receive from or contribute back to the LLC such reallocation or redistribution.

6.2.5 <u>Restrictions Relating to LLC Capital</u>: Except as otherwise specifically provided in this Agreement, no Member shall have the right to withdraw or reduce his or her Capital Contribution; no Member shall be entitled to receive interest on his or her Capital Contribution; no Member shall have the right to partition of LLC property or to receive property other than cash, if any, in return for his or her Capital Contribution; no Member shall be required to make any further contributions to the Capital of the LLC; except as otherwise provided herein, no Member shall be liable to the LLC or to any other Person to restore any deficit balance in his or her Capital Account or to reimburse any other Member for any portion of such other Member's investment in the LLC; no Member shall have priority over any other member as to the return of his or her Capital Contribution; and no Member shall have a right to the return of his or her Capital Contribution prior to dissolution and termination of the LLC, and then only to the extent of Cash Available For Distribution.

6.2.6. <u>Nature of LLC Interest</u>: Interests shall be personal property for all purposes. All property owned by the LLC, whether real or personal, tangible or intangible, shall be deemed to be owned by the LLC as an entity; and no Member, individually, shall have ownership of such property. The Members hereby agree that no Member, nor any successor in interest to any Member, shall have the right while this Agreement remains in effect, to have any LLC asset partitioned, or to file a complaint or institute any proceedings at law or in equity to have such asset partitioned; and each Member, on behalf of himself, his or her successors, successor-in-title, and assigns, hereby waves any such right.

Article VII
Term

7.1 The LLC shall continue in perpetuity. The LLC shall terminate due to events causing dissolution of the LLC under the laws of the State of Georgia.

Article VIII
Profits, Losses, and Distributions

8.1 <u>Operating Profits and Operating Losses</u>: For financial accounting, the LLC's net profits and losses will be computed in accordance with general accepted accounting principles, on an annual basis, and shall be allocated to the Member in proportion to Member's relative capital interest in the LLC as set forth in Schedule B. No Member has priority over any other Member as to LLC profits.

8.2 <u>Tax Allocation: Code Section 704(c)</u>: In accordance with Internal Revenue Code Section 704(c) and the Regulations there under income, gain, loss, and deduction with respect to any property contributed to the capital of the LLC shall, solely for tax purposes, be allocated among the Members so as to take account of any variation between the adjusted basis of such property to the LLC for federal income tax purposes and its initial Gross Asset Value. In the event the Gross Asset Value of any LLC asset is adjusted, subsequent allocations of income, gain, loss, and deduction with respect to such asset shall take account of any variation between the adjusted basis of such asset for federal income tax purposes and its Gross Asset Value in the same manner as under IRS Code Section 704(c) and the Regulations thereunder. Any decision relating to such allocations shall be made by the Manager in any manner that reasonably reflects the purpose and intention of this Agreement. Allocations pursuant to this Section are solely for purposes of federal, state, and local taxes and shall not affect, or in any way be taken into account in computing, any Member's Capital Account or share of Profits, Losses, other items or distributions pursuant to any provision of this Agreement.

8.3 <u>Distributions</u>: The Member shall determine and distribute available funds at frequent intervals as the Member sees fit. Available funds, as referred to herein, shall mean the net cash of the LLC available after appropriate provision for expenses and liabilities, as determined by the Member. Distributions in liquidation of the LLC shall be made in accordance with the positive capital account balance, in accordance to such Members' percentage interest, pursuant to Internal Revenue Code, Treasury Regulations.

Article IX
Expenses and Compensation of the Manager

9.1 <u>Manager Compensation</u>: Manager rendering services to the LLC shall be entitled to compensation commensurate with the value of such services, whether as consultant independent contractor, or other so long as such compensation is reasonable and in conformance with Internal Revenue Code Section 4975(d) and/or Department of Labor PTE 96-62.

9.2 <u>Expense Reimbursement</u>: The Member and/or Manager shall be entitled to incur any and all costs, overhead, and expenses so long as such expenses are necessary and ordinary for the LLC's production of income, and the member and/or manager does not receive any incidental benefit from the expenses. The LLC shall reimburse the Member and/or Manager for all direct out-of-pocket expenses incurred in managing the Company.

Article X
Management of the LLC, Powers, and Obligations of the Manager

10.1 <u>Manager</u>: The Manager of the LLC shall be (your name here)

10.2 <u>Restrictions of Authority of the Manager</u>: Except as otherwise specifically provided in this Agreement, the Manager shall not have the right to perform any act in violation of any applicable law, the regulations thereunder, or to perform any act this is inconsistent with the terms of this Agreement. In particular, the Manager does not have the power or authority to enter into any actions that would be considered prohibited transactions as per Internal Revenue Code Section 4975(e)(1). However, Manager is authorized pursuant to Department of Labor PTE 96-62 to rely on EXPRO exemptions for specific transactions. Manager has the authority to conduct any and all business transactions of the LLC collectively or individually.

10.3 <u>Devotion of Time</u>: The Manager shall manage and control the LLC and its business to the best of Manager's ability, but in so doing, the Manager shall devote only such time to the business of the LLC as is reasonably required to discharge their duties.

10.4 <u>Manager's Right to Deal with the LLC</u>: Manager shall not contract with or otherwise deal with the LLC. In the event it is deemed in the best interests of the LLC to engage in a transaction with any entity in which a disqualified person as defined in Internal Revenue Code Section 4975 has any ownership interest, the transaction must be analyzed and approved by an individual who is not related (as per Internal Revenue Code Section 267(c) to any Member or Manager of the LLC. This limitation however is governed by both the Internal Revenue Code Section 4975(d) and Department of Labor PTE 96-62, and Manager, any entity controlling, controlled by, under common control with, or otherwise affiliated with Manager shall rely on Internal Revenue Code Section 4975(d) and/or Department of Labor EXPRO when determining the validity of a transaction.

Article XI
Removal of Manager

11.1 <u>Death or Incapacity of Manager</u>: In the event of death or incapacity of Manager, the LLC shall be dissolved. Upon dissolution, the LLC must pay its debts first before distributing cash, assets, and/or initial capital to the Member's estate or interests.

11.2 <u>Bankruptcy, Other Circumstances, and Involuntary Assignment by Manager</u>: In the event the Manager's Interest is taken by levy, foreclosure, charging order, execution, or other similar proceeding, the LLC shall not dissolve. The assignee of the Manager's Interest shall receive only that Manager's rights to distributions or profits and losses of the LLC and shall, in no event, have the right to interfere in the management or the administration of the LLC business or affairs or to act as a Manager. The assignee shall only have the right to receive profits and losses attributable to the Manager's Interest in the LLC, and shall not be admitted as a Member or Manager of the LLC. In this event, Manager may elect to dissolve the LLC.

Article XII
Assignment of LLC Interests

12.1 <u>Assignment</u>: In accordance with the laws governing the State of Georgia, should the Member have a creditor with a judgment that was issued an assignment of the membership interest, the creditor shall only obtain an assignment of the membership interest, not the actual transfer of Membership in the LLC. The new assignee does not have any rights of the Member or have the ability to be involved in management of the LLC or the right to dissolve the LLC. The new assignee is only granted rights of the distributions of the Member's interests, if the Member decides to distribute at all, not the rights of membership. The assignee must release the Member's interests back to Member upon payment of the judgment in accordance with appropriate Court.

Article XIII
Dissolution, Winding-up and Termination

<u>Dissolution of the LLC</u>: The LLC shall be dissolved upon the first of any of the following events to occur:

13.1.1 The Member may dissolve the LLC at any time. Upon dissolution the LLC must pay its debts first before distributing cash, assets, and/or initial capital to the Member or the Member's interests.

13.1.2 The retirement, death, bankruptcy, or insanity of the Manager.

13.1.3 The disposition of all, or substantially all, of the property of the LLC, including, without limitation, cash and assets.

<u>Winding-up and Termination</u>: If, upon dissolution, the Member elects to wind up the LLC or fail to continue its business, the Manager (or if there is no Manager, their designated interest, heir or assigned probate of the State) shall take only those steps necessary to wind up the LLC's business and, in connection therewith, shall take full account of the LLC's assets and liabilities, and such assets or the proceeds therefrom shall be applied in the following order:

13.2.1 To the payment and discharge of all the LLC debts and liabilities to Persons other than Members

13.2.2 To the payment and discharge of LLC debts and liabilities to Members (or former members)

13.2.3 To the payment and discharge of LLC debts and liabilities to Manager (or former Manager)

13.2.4 To those Members (or their designated interests, heir) with positive balances in their Capital Accounts, in the ratio of such positive balance until no Member shall have a positive Capital Account

Article XIV
Accounting and Tax Record Considerations

14.1 <u>Accounting</u>: The LLC's books and records shall be maintained at the Company's principal place of business. Such books and records shall be maintained on that method of accounting selected by the Manager. The fiscal year of the LLC shall be the calendar year, or any other date so approved, and accepted by the Internal Revenue Service.

14.2 <u>Tax on Unrelated Business Income</u>: In accordance with Internal Revenue Code Section 512, if it is determined that income from a trade or business carried on by the LLC is to substantially related to the performance by the LLC of operating for the exclusive benefit of and deriving income for the exclusive benefit of the member and/or its beneficiaries Manager will compile any and all information and/or documentation necessary to timely file IRS Form 990-T and Manager shall pay any such tax due in full upon filing of the 990-T, but no later than the return is due, as determined without extensions. Manager shall make estimated tax payments if it is expected that any unrelated income tax after allowable adjustments will be in excess of $500.00.

14.3 <u>Tax on Income from Debt Financed Property</u>: In determining the LLC's tax liability, if any, Manager shall include any investment income that would otherwise be excluded from an exempt organization's unrelated business taxable income if such income is derived from debt-financed property pursuant to Internal Revenue Code Section 514. If, after accounting for all deductions and exemptions granted by Internal Revenue Code Section 514, Manager determines the LLC will owe tax, Manager shall compute tax in accordance with previously stated code and Manager will pay such tax due in full, no later than the return is due.

Article XV
Rights and Obligations of Members

15.1 <u>Management of Business</u>: The Members shall not take part in the management or control the business of the LLC nor transact any business in the name of the LLC. The Members shall not have the power to sign for or bind the LLC to any agreement or document. The Members shall not have any liability with respect to the LLC and the Members hereof, nor any power or authority with respect to the LLC except as stated elsewhere in this Agreement.

15.2 <u>Limitation on Liability of the Members</u>: The liability of each Member shall be limited to its Capital Contribution. No member shall have any additional personal liability to contribute money to or in respect of, the liabilities or obligations of the LLC. Members have no obligation to make advances to the LLC.

Article XVI
Miscellaneous

16.1 <u>Notices</u>: LLC notices, requests, demands, instruction, records, statements, returns or other communication required or permitted may be mailed to Members via regular first-class mail, postage prepaid or by electronic communication. Notice shall be deemed to have been given after mailing or transmission, to be five business days in the manner provided above. Unless and until such written notice is given, the last address given or provided herein (if no change has been given) shall control. Any communications or notices to the LLC shall be addressed to the Manager at the LLC's principal place of business.

16.3 <u>Section Captions</u>: Section and other captions contained in this

Agreement are for reference purposes only and are in no way intended to describe, interpret, define or limit the scope, extent or intent of this Agreement or any provisions hereof.

16.4 Severability: Every provision of this Agreement is severable. If any provision hereof is held to be illegal or invalid for any reason whatsoever, such illegality or invalidity shall not affect the validity of the remainder of this Agreement.

16.5 Amendments: Amendments to this Agreement may be proposed by the Manager or Members. The manager shall give notice to the Members of any proposed amendment. A proposed amendment shall have required response of no less than fifteen days and failure to response will constitute a vote in favor of the recommendation. The Manager may, without the consent of any Member, amend this Agreement or any of the documents or agreements executed only for the purpose of:

16.5.1 Correcting an error or omission;

16.5.2 Satisfying the requirements of the conditions imposed by any federal or state governmental agency with jurisdiction over the LLC or any requirements of the IRS

16.6 The Manager will not be required to amend the Certificate more than once each calendar year.

16.7 Right to Rely on the Authority of the Manager: No person dealing with the Manager shall be required to determine their authority to make any commitment or undertaking on behalf of the LLC, or to determine any fact or circumstance bearing upon the existence of their authority. In addition, no purchaser of any asset owned by the LLC shall be required to determine the sole and exclusive authority of the Manager to sign and deliver on behalf of the LLC any instrument of transfer; or to confirm the application or distribution of revenues or proceeds paid or credit in connection therewith, unless such purchasers shall have received written notice from the LLC to the contrary.

16.8 <u>Litigation</u>: The LLC and the Manager shall respond to any final decree, judgment, or decision of a court of competent jurisdiction or board or authority having jurisdiction in the matter. The LLC shall satisfy any such judgment decree, or decision first out of any insurance proceeds available therefrom next out of the capital and assets of the LLC.

16.9 <u>Applicable Law</u>: The laws of the state of Georgia shall govern the interpretation of this Agreement.

16.10 <u>Assurance</u>: Each Member agrees to execute such further documents and to co-operate fully with other Members in taking whatever further action may be necessary or appropriate to effectuate the purposes of this Agreement.

16.11 <u>Authority</u>: Each individual executing this Agreement warrants that he or she is authorized to do so and that the execution and performance of this Agreement by such person does not violate any Agreement or legal restriction to which such person is subject and that this Agreement will constitute a legally binding obligation.

Article XVII
Signatures of Members and Managers

IN WITNESS WHEREOF, the Member of this LLC, and the Manager on the date of execution of this Agreement, sign and adopt this agreement as the Operating Agreement of this LLC and agree to abide by its terms.

MANAGER:____

PRINT NAME:____

SIGNATURE:___________________________________DATE__________

MEMBER:

The xyz co

Custodian FBO (Your Name Here) IRA

Address

Address

Tax ID:

SIGNATURE:_______________________________DATE___________

Schedule A

Xyz co

<u>MANAGER:</u>

Name and address

<u>MEMBER:</u>

Xyz co

Custodian (FBO name) IRA (your number here)

Address:

Tax ID:

Interest: 100%

Capital %: 100%

Schedule B
Capital Contribution Ledger

The xyz co Custodian FBO name IRA

Amount of Contribution ______Date _____________

Amount of Contribution ______Date _____________

Amount of Contribution ______Date _____________

Amount of Contribution ______Date _____________

Amount of Contribution ______Date _____________

STEP 5

SUBMITTING YOUR OPERATING AGREEMENT FOR REVIEW

Now that you've got your Operating Agreement completed, you'll need to submit a copy of it to your selected trust holder (as earlier stated, Kingdom Trust was mine) for them to review and accept it while you just wait around for several days with baited breath hoping for something like this...

Great News!

They accepted this version of mine on the first go round so I was good to go and set up my account with them. They sent me documents to fill out, including an Account Adoption Agreement where I had to name any beneficiaries for the account, specifically what type of account did I want (traditional IRA) and how much my initial contribution into the account was going to be. I paid the annual account fee of about $100 and was issued an account number.

6

STEP 6

MOVING MONEY!

Now how to get the money from my existing 401k account at Merrill Lynch to Kingdom Trust? I had to contact Merrill Lynch and request rollover to my new account at Kingdom Trust. Merrill Lynch closed my account and sent all funds payable to me, but they were overnighted to Kingdom Trust address, via check. That is their specific practice. Kingdom Trust will accept wire or check delivery. Merrill Lynch wouldn't send wire. Kingdom Trust notified me immediately upon receipt and so there sat my money. Now what? So just what makes this IRA self-directed, you ask? How do I get my hands on it to invest it?

STEP 7

SET UP A BUSINESS BANK ACCOUNT

You must set up a business bank account. Verify that your bank of choice allows such accounts. My credit union didn't and I learned during this process that usually only national bank do. I chose Wells Fargo and have enjoyed good service with them. You can actually do this after Step 5, if you'd like. To open the acount, you will need:

1. Filed Articles of Organization which you will receive directly from the State in Step 1.
2. EIN confirmation from the IRS that you received in Step 2.
3. Operating Agreement – the one I saved you many headaches on.
4. About $100 bucks to open the account (or whatever the bank you chose requires).
5. The bank account must be opened in the name of the LLC. You can get a debit card for the account. You CANNOT get a credit card because that would require that you personally co-sign to guarantee it. As a prohibited party with such a business set up as this example is, you are not legally allowed to do this. You can obtain checks for the

account. The account name is the LLC and your name can appear below that as Manager

Note that ANYTHING that goes through this account must be directly related to legitmate asset purchases and concur with the IRS tax guidelines for the type of business you are operating. This isn't free reign to head to Vegas and start gambling. Uncle Sam will be after you in no time.

8

———

STEP 8

START INVESTING!

If you don't already know, now's the time to know exactly what assets you wish to purchase with those funds. Since I'm into real estate, I wanted to buy a house to flip. I submitted an Investment Direction request to my provider, Kingdom Trust, to transfer my funds into my business account. In turn I was then able to show proof of funds for a cash offer to a seller on a property, closed on it in a couple weeks and I was officially an investor in charge of my own IRA. Fast forward through renovations and subsequent sale of the home at a substantial profit and those funds were then used to make another home purchase. I now do not have to worry about my retirement. I can flip these houses or rent them out to qualifying individuals while watching my investment grow. My money is now earning its keep no longer wallowing in some portfolio stock choices that others make for me.

9

CONGRATULATIONS...YOU DID IT!

Sounds pretty simple, huh? I'm here to tell you it actually is. Just know that any earned income on your properties with this set up example must be reinvested and is not yours to keep and spend friendly. Keep good records and pay yourself when you successfully retire. You can hire a tax accountant and lawyer to do all this set up for you but the fact is, you don't have to. If your company gets to big to handle a few years down the road, you most certainly should engage the services of such professionals to keep your business on the up and up as you expand and utilize the services of a tax accountant when filing each year.

Work smarter, not harder, and have fun with your business start up!